Iva Polansky
The War of the Tolstoys

A Biographic Novella

© 2018 by Iva Polansky
Editing by Margaret Pollex
Cover design: Iva Polansky
ISBN-13: 978-1535111812
ISBN-10: 153511181X

Table of Contents

Part One: The Monster is back……………………...………..1
Part Two: The War of the Diaries……………………..…….22
Part Three: The Promise……………………………………..48
Part Four: The Big Cleaning………………...………………60
Part Five: The Flight………………………………………...73
Part Six: The Terminus………………………………………84

Tolstoy Quotes………………………………...…………….92

Lunch at Yasnaya Polyana, circa 1905. This photo shows the principal actors of the drama. Seated at the left are Dr. Makovitsky, Sasha, unknown, Chertkov, Leo Tolstoy, and Sonya. First on the right is Varya

"All happy families are alike; each unhappy family is unhappy in its own way."
Leo Tolstoy

The author of the above quote founded a family that was unhappy in many ways for the Tolstoys were strong-willed individuals with conflicting ideas of what was right. Life with a genius is never easy, and it was true for Sophia (Sonya) Tolstoy. Past his middle age, her husband turned to sainthood and, with the help of his so-called best friend, Vladimir Chertkov, founded a simple-living philosophy that attracted thousands of followers around the world. The disturbing communist ideas displeased the ruling class. From philosophical to political, Tolstoy's pamphlets were printed in England and smuggled to Russia. Famous and respected, Leo Tolstoy was untouchable but the authorities kept an eye on him and his collaborators, some of whom were imprisoned or sent to exile.

For the first half of his life, Leo was an aristocrat with all the privileges that went with his title. He was also Russia's most successful author: his novels *War and Peace* and *Anna Karenina* became international classics. Sonya, his loyal life companion, acted as his editor, his secretary, and his estate manager as well as his ever-pregnant wife. Sixteen pregnancies and thirteen births resulted in seven living children at the time of Leo's death. Her children's future was Sonya's priority. With her husband renouncing his worldly possessions in her favour, she was the guardian of the family estate as well as the manager of his copyrighted material written before 1881. The royalties, she hoped, would support the family in the future. Vladimir Chertkov, Tolstoy's publisher, intended otherwise. The resulting war between Chertkov and Sonya, in which the aged Leo was a pawn, is told on the following pages.

Part One
The Monster is Back

A steady rain drums on tree branches. The woods surrounding the Yasnaya Polyana mansion echo with numerous distant calls. Close by, a rustle of leaves and a cracking of twigs warn Sonya Tolstoy of approaching searchers. A moan and a sob will draw them close. Nothing too dramatic is needed, just enough noise to catch their attention.

It has worked.

"Did you hear that? She's here somewhere," says the wobbly tenor voice of Dr. Makovitsky. "Sophia Andreyevna? Where are you?"

"Mama? Mama, answer me!"

Not you, Sasha. I don't want to see you. Neither you nor that puny Slovak doctor. Where's Leo? Leo is supposed to look for me. The rest of you go home.

Too late. There is a swish of branches as someone forces a passage through the bushes next to the prostrate figure. The stout daughter leans over Sonya and sets her hands on her hips.

"Mama! What on earth are you doing?"

"I'm dying in the ditch according to your father's wishes."

The voice is mournful. The head rests on crossed arms for a dramatic effect.

Sasha is not impressed. "What nonsense! He never said such a thing. Let's get you up!"

With Dr. Makovitsky's help, she pulls her mother to her feet. The latter, wet and bedraggled, opens the floodgate of her frustration.

"Your father doesn't have to state the obvious," she wails. "He simply doesn't care. Did he ever bother to ask how I manage to keep food on the table while he's working for free? He will not be content until the whole family ends up begging by the roadside." Tears have come now. They are rolling down the cheeks, washing the collection of wrinkles written by sixty-eight years of life. "I'm old and weary. I can no longer take care of everything."

Sasha and Makovitsky hustle the distraught woman along the path leading to the mansion. They are nearing the back porch and have already been spotted by other searchers.

"They've found the Countess. Call off the search!" The message is repeated by different callers. It is decreasing in volume as it is being conveyed to the far end of the woods.

"I beg you to control yourself, Sophia Andreyevna," the doctor says as they approach the steps. "Your tantrums undermine your husband's health."

Sonya turns on him with a vicious snarl. "And which husband are you talking about, Doctor? He wears so many hats. The aristocratic peasant? The hunting vegetarian? The saintly atheist? Or do you mean the champion of celibacy who put me in childbed thirteen times?"

The daughter is offended. "You don't respect his greatness!"

"I respect the novelist, not the pamphleteer."

This is too good a line for the doctor to let go. Surreptitiously, he reaches into his jacket, and his hand begins to wiggle inside the pocket.

"Stop it! Stop scribbling in your pocket!"

The guilty hand is quickly withdrawn. "Sophia Andreyevna, I assure you..."

"What's this then?" Sonya has reached into his pocket and is now brandishing several three by five cards and a stub of pencil. She flings the cards at him.

Sasha voices her disapproval. "Well, really, Doctor! You know that Father hates this. Why can't we have a moment of privacy?"

The porch door creaks and a white-bearded peasant steps out. His wife rushes up the steps, her eyes teary again.

"Leo. . . Lyovochka, my love! Why are you driving me mad?"

Down on his knees, Dr. Makovitsky begins to gather the scattered cards. He knows that every preserved word is worth gold.

A horse-drawn wagon rattles through the gate-posts of the mansion. Seated at the back, his legs dangling, a young man keenly observes the hustle and bustle of the courtyard. A gaggle of geese is crossing the path of a servant puffing under the weight of a basket laden with wet laundry. A pair of carriage horses is led through the stable door. Sun-burned estate workers carrying scythes return from the fields. In the middle of the courtyard, sheltered under an oak tree, a gathering of dust-covered pilgrims gulps water from colorful jugs offered by a couple of maids. A group of city visitors, the women sporting oversized fashionable hats, have gathered in front of the main building. They are posing for a photograph.

The wagon halts. The young man jumps down and reaches for his suitcase.

In the office, a typewriter clatters as Sasha pounds at the keys. A perky brunette bends her head over an account book. At her side, a grubby peasant stuffs mail into a leather bag when someone knocks at the door.

Sasha keeps typing. "Philichka, get the door!"

Philichka shuffles to the door and opens it a crack. After an unintelligible verbal exchange, he turns to Sasha. "There's a man who says he comes from Mr. Chertkov."

Sasha stops typing and gets up. "By all means, let him in! . . . You must be the new secretary," she greets the new arrival enthusiastically. "Come in, come in!"

The young man offers his hand. "Bulgakov, Valentin Fyodorovich."

The offered hand is shaken vigorously. "I'm Alexandra Leovna. You come highly recommended by Mr. Chertkov. How is he?"

"Bearing the exile with his customary bravery. I admire his dedication to the Tolstoyan cause."

"As we do all. My father is missing him terribly, I must say. I think that you'll spend a considerable time answering his questions about Mr. Chertkov's well-being. He feels guilty about the whole thing."

"He shouldn't. Mr. Chertkov feels privileged to suffer for the Master. I know I would."

Sasha shrugs. "I don't think you'll have time for suffering. We are overwhelmed. Tonight someone has to go to the station to pick up a delegation from the Tolstoyan community in the Caucasus and a couple of Japanese journalists." Noticing that Philichka, the mailbag over his shoulder, is about to leave, she asks him to wait for one more letter. "Varya, dear," she calls the perky brunette, 'show Valentin Fyodorovich around." Turning back to Bulgakov, she explains, "Miss Feokritov is my mother's secretary." The introduction made, she returns to the typewriter and resumes her work.

Varya takes up her task with a smile. "We are a bit stretched," she says during the handshake. "Summer is a busy time." She motions toward a door. "Leo Nikolayevich's study. No one is allowed in while he works. Alexandra Leovna copies everything he writes and sends it to Mr. Chertkov, who sees to the publishing and translation. I work for the countess, who manages the copyright for anything written before 1881. As for your work . . ." She leads him to a desk piled high with correspondence.

"Excuse me, I just . . ." A nervous woman in a hat harboring a fantasy bird stands in the door. She holds an artfully wrapped gift box.

Sasha is furious. "Who left the door open? Deal with this, Varya!"

"What can I do for you?" Varya asks the visitor. "Are you lost?"

"Would it be possible to see Count Tolstoy just for a minute? I shall not bother him at all. I only mean to tell him how much I admire him."

The visitor has barely finished the last word when the study door opens, and Leo enters, holding a few sheets of paper.

"Sashenka, type these as well, please," he says.

At the sight of him the admirer swoons. Bulgakov leaps forward and catches her in his arms. Startled, Leo hands the sheets to Philichka, who is the closest, backs up into the study and shuts the door.

"Thank God you were here, Valentin Fyodorovich," Varya says. "Now you have seen what we have to deal with. This, too, is a part of your job."

Morning sun rays pour into a Spartan room containing a single iron cot with a crocheted bedcover. Plain peasant clothing hangs from hooks on the wall.

Leo pours sudsy water from his washbasin into a slops bucket.

In the corridor, there is a morning rush as maids carry towels and hot water for the household. Leo, hauling the slops bucket, leaves his room and blends in with the servants.

It's a bright summer day at Yasnaya Polyana. Chairs and tables are distributed on the lawn, where the Tolstoy clan enjoys a lazy afternoon. Leo, his children and their spouses, their children, guests, and dogs, all digest the Sunday lunch. Valets in white jackets and gloves carry trays with drinks and snacks.

Leo, incongruous in his peasant garb amidst all this elegance, looks like he is enjoying himself. He is seated at a table with his eldest daughter Tanya, with Sasha, and Dr. Makovitsky. Sasha rubs her poodle's belly. Makovitsky is examining a new dog leash.

"Oh, Alexandra Leovna," the doctor says, "are you not ashamed of yourself? Why buy from the Jews? Why don't you support your own?"

Leo chuckles. "Dushan, you are a saint. But since there are no true saints, God gave you one fault - the hatred of Jews." He notices a young man with Jewish features sauntering toward the table. "Ah, Goldenweiser! Come and sit down, Alyosha."

Subdued, Makovitsky forces a smile.

"There's been a conspiracy in your house, Leo Nikolayevich," Goldenweiser says. "But I'm bound by a promise of silence."

Intrigued, all look up to see Sonya followed by son Andrey who is carrying a phonograph.

"Surprise, surprise!" Sonya calls. "This came in the mail yesterday."

"What is it?" Leo asks.

Andrey sets the contraption on the table. "A gift from Mr. Edison, the inventor."

"It records music and voices," Sonya explains. "Fortunately, Andreyusha had seen one in Paris and knows how to operate it."

Andrey is winding the spring. "It's very simple. All you have to do is slip on a wax cylinder and put the needle down."

Music and a distorted soprano voice split the air to the ah's and oh's of a collective marvel. More people cluster around the table. Tanya seizes this opportunity to draw her father aside.

"Papushka, you must come to Kotchety." She leans closer to his ear. "Mr. Chertkov is back from exile."

Leo is greatly pleased. "Why didn't he write to me?" he asks, grinning.

"He didn't know until the last minute. His mother stirred up the matter and succeeded in bringing him back. Now he is waiting for the permit to settle at Telyatinki. He can't wait to see you. He's found lodgings near the border, only two miles from our estate." Tanya winks at her father. "Don't worry about Mama. I'll keep her busy."

"Tanya, Tanyechka, this is good news. Good news, indeed!"

In the tennis court, a ball is being batted between a balding middle-aged man and a female adversary. The loud plop, plop, as it hits the rackets blends in with the phonograph opera rendition from the lawn around the bend of the gravel path. Bulgakov, carrying two glasses, joins Varya on a bench facing the court.

He hands her a glass. "Your lemonade."

She nods her thanks and turns her attention to the game.

"I forgot. Which son is that?" Bulgakov asks.

"Leo Junior."

"Is he the one who published a book on the evils of Tolstoyism? The old man must have been very annoyed with him."

Varya laughs. "What rattled him the most was that his own son should do it with so little talent."

Returning to the lawn, Varya and Bulgakov each pick a cake from a tray. The opera production is at an end, replaced with loud screams and squeals as children spill out of the door, pursued by Sonya dressed as a witch.

Brandishing a broom, Sonya performs a little dance and the children are frantic with delight. Bulgakov observes the scene with a grave expression.

"Mr. Chertkov told me such terrible things about the countess. She's actually a very nice woman."

"Just wait," says Varya.

The sun has moved on, changing the shade of the trees. Leo sits with his youngest grandson asleep on his knee. He is observing the other children's antics. Sonya, her witch's attire replaced with a tea gown, walks out of the house and sits next to him.

"That was fun," Leo says.

Sonya smiles and stretches her arm. Leo clasps her hand in his. They sit in silence, allowing contentment to wash over them.

"Tanya says we should come over next week," Sonya says. "If it is not too much for you."

"I'm not dead yet."

"We'll go then."

She contemplates her brood. "Look at them. Aren't they beautiful?"

Leo nods.

"Your own flesh and blood," she continues. "If only you were reasonable!"

Leo rejects her hand. "Why do you have to spoil everything?" He casts a contemptuous look around. "Silverware and French poodles! What am I doing here?"

He hands the child to her and angrily stomps away.

"That's it! Run away from responsibility," Sonya shouts after him. "You cannot be bothered to care for your children. You'd rather play at sainthood."

The first morning at the Kotchety estate sees Sonya in her nightgown leaning out of the window, looking down at the courtyard, where Leo mounts a horse.

"Lyovochka, be careful with that horse! Where are you going?"

Ignoring her, Leo nudges his horse forward.

"He's gone riding, the old fool. Alone, on that horse," Sonya complains at the breakfast table she shares with Tanya's family and Dr. Makovitsky.

"He rides every day," Tanya says.

"That's at home. He doesn't know this horse. What if it throws him?"

Meanwhile, two miles away, her husband reins in his horse to consult a peasant. The peasant points in the direction of a wooden house. Minutes later, Leo arrives at the door.

"Volodya!" he shouts.

There's a moment of quiet before the door opens and Vladimir Chertkov appears. At fifty-seven, he is still an imposing and handsome man, elegant even in his peasant blouse.

Leo dismounts and they clasp each other in a bear-like embrace. Soon after, they stride along a path, both energized by the pleasure of each other's company.

"Mother applied pressure at the very top," Chertkov says. "I'll be allowed to stay at Telyatinki for the duration of her visit."

"Will she stay for long?"

Chertkov chuckles. "She has graciously agreed to stay indefinitely."

Leo pats his shoulder. They both laugh, and then Leo frowns. "Sonya has to be told."

"Has she been difficult lately?"

Leo sighs. "How I hate it all! Possessions, fine china. The guilt of living in luxury while millions starve. Every time I look in the mirror I see a despicable man."

Chertkov stops abruptly and puts his hands on Leo's shoulders. "You of all people must be allowed to live according to your principles. Pardon my frankness, Leo Nikolayevich, but I cannot stand by and watch Sophia Andreyevna poisoning the last years of your life. It's time to leave."

"No, that would kill her."

"In the meantime, she's killing you."

"She's my wife."

"God should've given you a wife like mine. Devoted, respectful, supportive."

They have resumed their stroll, and Chertkov attacks a more important problem. "What will happen to your spiritual legacy when you return to the Maker?" he asks. "You're over eighty, Leo Nikolayevich. The more you hesitate, the greater the danger of your work falling victim to Sophia Andreyevna's greed."

"What do you suggest?"

"The answer is a will. A proper, unbreakable will."

Leo ponders this proposition. "Sonya," he whispers.

"Naturally, we must act in secret. Should she find out while you're alive, she would spare you no peace. Find any pretext and come to Moscow. You and Alexandra Leovna."

"Sasha?"

"I believe that you can trust her. You need an ally."

"Sasha," Leo repeats thoughtfully.

The sun, having worked all day, is nearing the horizon for a rest. From the balcony at Kotchety, Sonya observes Leo, who is returning at a leisurely canter.

"I know you mean well," her daughter Tanya says. "You suffer when he eats badly, you try to save him from boring visitors, and you surround him with every possible care. At the same time, you lose sight of what he really needs."

Sonya turns to her. "What do you want me to do? Am I to move to a peasant hut and scrub the floor just to please him? What possible good would that achieve? I'm too old for such nonsense. And you! You used to be besotted with his ideas but I don't see any calluses on your hands.

In Leo's study, after the return to Yasnaya Polyana, Leo and Sasha stare at each other in silence.

"Have you thought it over?" Sasha asks at last. "That one million ruble offer for the rights to your collected works is what Mama's counting on. She'd fight such a will tooth and claw."

"I cannot back out. It's a gift to the people, the fulfillment of a sacred duty to God and man. May I count on your support?"

Sasha takes her father's hand in hers and gives it an affectionate squeeze.

Sonya sullenly observes the rush of departure as servants carry luggage through the front door. Sasha helps Leo with his overcoat while Dr. Makovitsky and Bulgakov button theirs.

"Wasting your time touring a madhouse!" Sonya grumbles.

"A progressive mental institution," says Leo patiently.

"Don't you get enough press attention? Do you need more?"

"Mama, we have been over this a hundred times. Don't start again."

"Oh, have your father to yourself, Sasha. Go! Go both of you! I know I'm no longer needed."

Sonya stomps through a door and slams it shut. Leo's face shows concern.

"Varya will take care of her," Sasha says soothingly.

Seated at a breakfast table set for two, Sonya is buttering a slice of bread, when Varya enters in a hurry, almost colliding with a departing maid.

"I'm sorry. I was sorting the mail."

Sonya lifts an eyebrow. "And a good morning to you."

Varya bends her head. "Sorry, good morning." She has a means of redemption. "A letter from Moscow!"

Sonya brightens instantly. Varya sits down to eat her breakfast while Sonya unfolds the letter and begins to read.

"Leo Nikolayevich is in good health and sleeps well . . . Ah! He's begun writing a short story. This is a good sign. Oh, Varya, could it be true? Is he about to abandon political pamphlets and return to fiction?"

Sonya reaches for the next page. She reads a few words and gasps.

"What? What is it?" Varya asks, alarmed.

"The monster is back."

Sonya leaps up and begins to pace the room. Varya stares at her, puzzled.

"Chertkov!" Sonya shouts. "Chertkov is back from the exile. He's returning to the Telyatinki farm. We'll have him on our doorstep, and it will start all over again. The manipulation, the plotting, the blackening of my character. Varya, you cannot understand. You were not here when this was going on. The man is pure evil."

She falls onto a chair. "Lyova's a coward. Instead of telling me, face to face, he writes. They are killing me, both of them. They are plotting as we speak. I know it. I feel it right here," she beats her chest. "Varya, send a telegram! 'Sophia Andreyevna's nerves are in bad shape. Insomnia. Weeping. Pulse one hundred and twenty. Return home immediately.' Go, Varya, go at once!"

The house is enlivened with the return of the Moscow party. Varya waits at the top of the staircase as luggage is being brought in and coats removed.

"How's she?" Leo asks.

Varya shakes her head.

"Papa, don't go up there!" Sasha pleads. "Let Dr. Makovitsky deal with her first. A few drops of laudanum . . ."

The doctor's face turns pale. "Last time she accused me of poisoning her."

"Then I will go," Sasha says.

Leo shakes his head. "That would make it even worse."

Bulgakov steps forward only to be rejected by all. Leo hands his coat to Sasha.

"Papushka, you're tired. Please don't!"

They watch with apprehension as Leo climbs the steps.

Leo cautiously opens the door of his wife's boudoir. A lamp casts a soft light over the comfortably furnished room decorated with icons and family photographs. Soft moans emanate from the bed, where Sonya buries her face in the pillows.

"Sonya?"

"Two days! It took you two days."

Sonya turns to face Leo and brings her hand from beneath the pillow, brandishing a crumpled telegram. "More convenient to come tomorrow. That's not your wording. It's Chertkov's. Perhaps it would have been more 'convenient' for him had I thrown myself under the train that was bringing you home. Like your Anna Karenina."

She begins to weep softly. "I have thought of that. I have! How easy it would be to leave it all behind, the entire struggle for the future of our children, all the worries, everything . . . I have a vial of opium. It's a very agreeable death. It allows one to peacefully exit this valley of tears. First sleepiness and then the end."

"Sonya, stop this nonsense, please."

"What happened to our love, Leo? Your letters from Moscow, they were all lies." She is sitting now, tears forgotten, anger distorting her features. "Don't imagine for one moment that I don't see through you!" she shouts. "It's all about Chertkov. You pretend to be affectionate to appease me while you revel in a pitiful senile love for that tsar's bastard."

Leo turns his back to her and heads for the door. Sonya jumps out of bed, runs after him, grabs his arm.

"You are a fool, Leo! Do you think he loves you? He loves only your glory. You are a national monument, and he is the self-appointed custodian. He enjoys his power over you, and that's the whole truth."

By now, Leo is seething. "I forbid you to speak of him in such terms. The man gave up everything for me. His wealth, his position in society, and even his freedom. He lives for the Tolstoyan cause body and soul, unlike me. I wallow in luxury because of you."

On the floor below, in the salon, Varya minds the samovar and distributes cups of tea as Sasha, Makovitsky, and Bulgakov, listen gloomily to the escalating quarrel above their heads. The men smoke nervously, while Sasha paces the room.

A thud of an overturned chair prompts Sasha into action. She heads for the door, the others following her lead.

Sonya, brandishing an opium vial, charges out of her room with Leo at her heels. They lock in a struggle for the vial. Leo succeeds in prying it out of her hand and throws it down the steps. The vial breaks under the feet of the rescue party. Bulgakov and Makovitsky pounce on Sonya, subduing her, while Sasha embraces her father.

Restrained by her captors, Sonya fights to reach Sasha. "It's your fault, traitor! Why did you sell Telyatinki to Chertkov? Why?" Giving up the struggle, she bursts into uncontrollable weeping. Uttering loud moans, she allows herself to be led back to her room.

Dawn dims the light of a lamp. Leo is stretched out on the bed, while Makovitsky massages his foot.

"That's enough, Dushan. I feel sleep coming. Go and get some rest yourself." Leo falls silent, listening. "How quiet the house is. Is she finally asleep? Did you give her a draft?"

The doctor covers Leo, tucking him in with tender care. "She's exhausted herself with weeping."

"Dushan?"

"Yes?"

"I think I must leave here. Would it be possible to arrange for a passport without anyone knowing?"

In the corridor, Sonya stands flattened against the wall as Makovitsky leaves Leo's room. She waits until the way is clear before approaching the door. She rests her forehead against it.

"Lyovochka?" she asks tenderly, her voice charged with guilt.

In his study, Leo signs the last letter of the day. "Anything else?" he asks. "Is that all for today?"

Bulgakov nods. "Yes, that's all."

"Make a copy of each for Vladimir Grigorievich's archives," says Leo. He notices Bulgakov's drawn features. "Are you all right?"

"Yes. I only suffer for you, Leo Nikolayevich."

"No, today it's all right, it's better. She said, 'You won't forgive me for all the things I have said about you', so she's aware of this . . . of her abnormality." Leo rubs his forehead. "Today I feel like a seventy-year-old."

"What do you mean? Is that good?"

"No, on the contrary. I cannot get used to the idea that I'm an old man."

Part Two
The War of the Diaries

Books, files, stacks of paper. Sonya inspects shelves and drawers in Leo's study. The search is becoming more and more frantic.

Outside, in the park, Leo is seated on a bench, surrounded by attentive listeners: a motley group of workers and intellectuals. Sonya exits the house and purposefully strides in their direction.

"I strongly disagree with mysticism," Leo says, unaware of his wife's approach. "Whatever is unclear is weak. It is the same in the field of ethics. Only those ethical truths that are clear—""

"Leo Nikolayevich, where are your diaries?" Sonya interrupts him rudely.

In his room, Leo lifts the pillow in the bed and reaches for a notebook. "Here it is. Are you content?"

Sonya extends her hand. "Show me what you have written about me!"

Reluctantly, Leo hands her the notebook. Sonya leafs through the latest entries.

"You write 'I must fight Sonya consciously, with kindness and love.' Why do you say you have to fight me? What have I done wrong?"

"Isn't it true that we disagree on the most basic principles?"

"That's only one notebook. Where is the rest? Where are the other forty-seven years of our life?"

Uneasy, Leo tightens lips and remains still for a while. "I don't know," he says at last.

Sonya stares at him.

"In a bank," he says.

It dawns on Sonya. "You gave them to Chertkov!"

Leo is silent. Sonya squeezes her head and screams.

It's moving day at the Telyatinki farm. Two wagons piled up with furniture and crates are being unloaded. The helpers, plainly dressed men and women, exude the self-denial and spiritual dedication befitting the Tolstoyan discipline followers. The elegance of Chertkov's aged mother stands out in the drab company. She is supervising the unloading of her personal effects: a crystal chandelier, carved furniture, Persian rugs, and other paraphernalia of luxury living.

The other wagon contains lackluster items. A crate is being lowered to the ground with a thud.

"Careful with those typewriters," Chertkov says.

"Vladimir Grigorievich! Welcome!"

Chertkov turns his head and smiles at the greeter. "Alyosha Goldenweiser! Good to see you."

They shake hands and slap each other's backs.

"So you've heard," Chertkov says.

"Everybody knows today is the day. Even the countess. For her, it was bad news."

A chuckle from Chertkov. "I should imagine."

"The situation in Yasnaya Polyana is rapidly deteriorating. Sophia Andreyevna raves about some diaries."

Chertkov shrugs. "Now that I'm here, I intend to patch up things." He sees another new arrival. "And here's young Bulgakov."

Bulgakov, smiling, pats a briefcase he is holding against his chest. "First batch of documents delivered in person. From now on, no more postage expenses. Welcome to Telyatinki, Vladimir Grigorievich!"

Chertkov accepts his hand without enthusiasm. "I need to talk to you."

The three have moved into Chertkov's new office. With a frown, he studies the contents of Bulgakov's briefcase.

"Valentin Fyodorovich, you have been provided with a special carbon notebook for your observations of the Tolstoy household. We had an understanding that the copies of your diary would be mailed to me each week. You complied for a while, but then the reports stopped coming. I expect an explanation."

Bulgakov's cheeks flush as he gathers courage. "I consulted my conscience and concluded that such activity is, in fact, spying," he answers. "I'm sorry, Vladimir Grigoriyevich, but I cannot act unethically."

"I see," Chertkov says, his voice made of ice. "Are you aware that you are betraying our cause? The Tolstoyan cause!"

"Not in the least. Leo Nikolayevich himself wouldn't agree with such an interpretation."

There is not an argument that would beat this. "Very well," Chertkov retreats. "Far be it from me to trample on your conscience. Well, this is a busy day as you well know. I'll see you tomorrow."

"The boy's a disappointment," Chertkov says to Goldenweiser when they are alone. "He's no longer to be trusted. I'll replace him with Strakhov."

"That would be difficult if not impossible. Leo Nikolayevich has developed a fatherly affection for him."

Chertkov shrugs. "Problems must be solved in the order of priority. The first obstacle is the wife."

At Yasnaya Polyana, a guest is expected.

"He's coming in the spirit of reconciliation," Leo says. "All I'm asking of you is to be civil."

"And all I'm asking you, begging you, is to reclaim the diaries," answers Sonya.

Sasha is at the end of her patience. "Do we have to go over it again? Papa has made a promise, haven't you, Papushka?"

The noise of horse's hooves beating the ground sets everyone on edge. Sasha approaches the door and pauses, hand on the handle. "Mama, please, try to be calm!" She opens the door and disappears into the hall. "Vladimir Grigorievich, welcome!" they hear her saying. "Papa's impatient to see you. And Mother too, I'm sure."

In her chair, Sonya snorts and rolls her eyes.

"Alexandra Leovna, what a pleasure!" The hated voice enters the room, preceding the man. Leo approaches the guest with an outstretched hand. They exchange a wordless emotional handshake followed by a hug.

"Sophia Andreyevna, your servant," Chertkov bends over Sonya to kiss her hand. "I have heard that you've recently been speaking of me as your enemy. This feeling must be attributed to some misunderstanding that will soon dissolve like a bad dream."

Sonya removes her hand from his and ostensibly rubs it against her skirt. There is an awkward moment before Leo intervenes. He hooks his hand under Chertkov's arm.

"Come Volodya, let's talk about old times." He leads the visitor to a sofa at the other side of the room.

"Ring for the tea, Sasha!" Sonya says.

Tea has been served. Sonya pretends to play solitaire while straining her ears and casting sly looks at the two men in intimate conversation.

Sasha enters, carrying a file. "The newspaper clippings. You will find them interesting, Vladimir Grigorievich."

Sonya's gaze is fixed on Leo's and Chertkov's knees: they are touching. She reaches for her teacup and deliberately drops it on the floor. The sound of breaking china interrupts the conversation. The air thickens as Leo and Sonya lock eyes.

"There is so much more I want to show you, Vladimir," Leo says a little too loudly. "Why don't we go to my study? Come with us, Sashenka, you know where everything is."

The atmosphere in the study is one of conspiracy as the talk is being led in hushed voices.

"Unfortunately, I was told that the term 'the people" is not legal," Chertkov says. "To make the will valid, you must bequeath your work to a specific person." He reaches into his breast pocket and unfolds the document. "At my request, the lawyer's made an alteration. I suggested Alexandra Leovna as the beneficiary and myself as the executor."

Sasha is terrified. "No, not me!"

"Alexandra Leovna, you alone understand the moral importance of your father's legacy."

"Will you do it, Sashenka?" Leo asks.

Sasha shakes her head. "Do you realize what you are asking? The family will tear me apart!"

"This from a woman whose strong will and dedication are admired by all who count in this matter?" Chertkov knows how to massage Sasha's ego. "Think of the sacrifices your father has been practicing all these years! Has he not renounced all his worldly goods? Has he not given his house and land to his wife? Should he go to his grave knowing that his humanitarian ideas will earn money for people who scorn his moral values?"

In the corridor, Sonya tiptoes toward the door.

In the study, Chertkov explains to Sasha his plans for the Tolstoy legacy. "You, as the beneficiary, will continue your father's work by releasing it into the public domain and I shall be at your side to guide you through the process."

Ear pressed to the door, Sonya listens, but all she can hear is a low murmur of voices. As her frustration grows, she bursts into the room.

"What are you talking about?" she shouts. "Is this another plot against me?"

Frightened, Leo clutches at his chest. Sasha throws her arms around him. "What are you doing? Do you want to kill him?"

Sonya points at Chertkov. "This is between that man and me."

Chertkov stands up, while Sasha whisks Leo out of the room. The two adversaries eye one another. A rapid fire follows.

"Countess?"

"Where are the diaries and what right do you have to keep them?"

"And what right do you have to interfere between master and disciple?"

"I'm asking you to return the diaries and to stop driving a wedge between husband and wife."

Chertkov's lips stretch to a crooked smile. "What are you afraid of, Sophia Andreyevna? That I shall use the diaries to unmask you? Had I wanted to, I could have ruined you and your family too. The only thing that has stopped me is my affection for your husband. Truly, if I had a wife like you, I'd blown my brains out a long time ago, or gone to America!"

With an angry stride, he leaves the room and slams the door.

Sonya is awakened by muffled moans. She sits up and listens. The moans continue. She slips out of bed and lights a candle. Carrying the candleholder, she follows the noise to Leo's bedroom. She opens the door to reveal a horrifying scene.

Kneeling on the bed, beads of sweat glistening on his forehead, Chertkov is sodomizing Leo. Fixing his diabolic gaze on Sonya, he laughs provocatively. Sonya drops the candleholder and flees, pursued by Chertkov's echoing laughter.

Sonya screams and wakes with a start. She rises, panting, and listens to the silence.

A beam of light appears under the door of Leo's bedroom. The door opens revealing Sonya clutching a candleholder. She stands on the threshold, inquisitively looking at her sleeping husband,

and then silently closes the door. The sound of her retreating steps blends in with Leo's regular breathing.

A carriage stops in front of the house, discharging Leo Junior and his luggage. That night, the visitor sits at the dinner table with his parents and with Sasha, Varya, Dr. Makovitsky, Bulgakov, and Goldenweiser. The conversation is about madness.

"I don't believe in madness nor do I excuse it," Leo says. "At the heart of every insane case, there's extreme egocentrism. People who are considered mad simply don't understand the needs of anybody except their own."

Sonya has been fidgeting all evening, and her restlessness has reached the limit. "Could we change the subject?" she asks.

Leo frowns. "Why?"

"Just change the subject please."

"We're just discussing my article."

"It bothers me, and you know it."

"Perhaps you see an allusion to yourself in it?"

Tension grips the room. Leo Junior looks from one parent to another. "What is this?"

"They all think I'm mad," Sonya says. "And it's true. Your father's driving me mad. But before I sink into madness for good, I must tell the truth. Leo Nikolayevich has an unnatural relationship with Chertkov."

There is an arrest of breathing, the refusal of understanding, the hope for an error in hearing.

"Don't deny it, Leo!" Sonya forges on. "The tendency has always been there. I remember that passage in your diary some fifty years ago. Dyakov was his name, wasn't it?"

Leo rises from his seat. "Get out! Get out of my house!" he thunders.

"It's my house now."

A pause follows, stiff with general consternation.

Leo stomps out of the room, followed by Dr. Makovitsky and Sasha. Just as she is about to leave the room, Sasha returns to the table and spits in her mother's face.

"Tell her that if she meant to kill me, she's succeeding," Leo says to Sasha as Dr. Makovitsky checks his pulse.

"The pulse is very uneven," the doctor says.

They are in Leo's bedroom, with the old man stretched out on the bed.

"Sasha . . . "

"Yes, Papenka?"

"Everything . . . My writing, my personal papers and translations, everything ever written by me, will go to you. And I mean everything, including the copyrights your mother has been managing."

"I'll make myself worthy of it, Papa."

"And one more thing. Promise me that after your mother's death you will buy this house and land from your siblings and turn it over to the peasants."

Sonya, dressed in her nightgown, eyes red from weeping, circles her bedroom. She kneels in front of an icon and prays.

In his bedroom, Leo stares at the ceiling. He hears the creaking of the floor planks as someone approaches. There is a light knock on the door.

"Lyovochka? Are you asleep?"

"Go away," Leo says wearily.

The door handle clicks and rattles. The room is locked.

"Lyovochka, you must forgive me!"

Leo pulls the bedcover over his head while Sonya continues rattling the door handle.

"Lyovochka, my love, I did not mean to anger you. But what else can I think if you behave as you do? Open the door and tell me none of what I said is true. Return the diaries and I'll believe you! . . . Leo? Lyovochka? Why don't you speak to me? . . . Leo? Speak to me! . . .   I'm kneeling in front of your door, Leo. Kneeling, begging. Say that Chertkov means nothing to you! Say that the diaries belong to your family!"

More rattling of the door.

Leo sits up in his bed. "You'll get nothing from me, nothing! Go away, woman! Go! Disappear!"

There is a silence before Sonya speaks. "So you are driving me away? Out of my home? I'm going then, never to come back. I'll die out there like a dog. Like a dog!"

The door of the guest room is open. Standing at the threshold, Dr. Makovitsky is holding a lantern, while Leo is bending over his son's bed.

"Lyova! Lyova, wake up!"

Leo's son stirs. "Father? What is it?"

"Your mother's left the house. It's been more than an hour now."

"Left? Why?"

"She's out there on the lawn. I want you and Dushan to bring her back."

The windows project rectangles of light on the lawn, where Sonya, clad in a nightgown, is stretched out on her stomach, her arms apart as if nailed to a cross. A light moves across the lawn as Leo Junior and Dr. Makovitsky approach the prostrate white form.

Leo Junior squats at her side and a discussion follows. Both men clutch Sonya's arms and pull her up. She fights them off and, again, stretches out on the grass. Leo Junior reasons with her. Another attempt at pulling her to her feet, another fight with the same result.

The men retrace their steps.

"She's not coming back unless you go out there and ask her to return," Leo Junior says to his father. "She says that you've put her out like a dog."

"No, you go back. Don't leave her alone."

"She wants you to come. Damn it, Papa, how can you stay in bed while your wife is out there, shivering with cold on the wet grass? Don't you think it's time to admit some responsibility for the state she's in? You'll go to her even if I have to drag you!"

In the hall, the household is watching as Sonya, wrapped in a blanket, is being led home by Leo, his arm around her shoulders. Despite her bedraggled state, she displays a victorious smile.

A crew of estate workers scythes hays in the afternoon heat. Some of them exchange a hand wave with Bulgakov, who is strolling down the road with his briefcase casually held over his shoulder. A noise of beating hooves and the rattle of wheels behind him grow and, soon, he is overtaken by a carriage. The vehicle stops and a smiling Sonya leans out.

"Valentin Fyodorovich, are you going to Telyatinki?"

"Why, yes, Sophia Andreyevna."

"In that case, may I offer you a ride?"

Bulgakov has a hard time hiding his lack of enthusiasm. "I . . . that is. . . Yes, thank you."

Inside the carriage he wedges himself into the corner, the briefcase locked in his arms. "Are you going to Telyatinki as well?" he asks.

"I'm taking tea with Mrs. Chertkov."

"She's a very gracious lady. That is . . .   as far as I know."

"She's my only hope," Sonya says in a liquid voice.

Bulgakov watches with dismay as the countess's carefully constructed façade crumbles: her shoulders sagging, the corners of her lips down.

She grasps his hand. "Help me. Please, help me!"

At forty-seven, Sergey is the oldest son. Now seated in the Yasnaya Polyana salon, he listens to his siblings Tanya and Leo Junior.

"Well, that's the situation in a nutshell and now it's your turn to take over," Leo Junior says. "Try to persuade father to give her the diaries because that's the only way to calm her. I'm not sure how much abuse she can take before her mind caves in."

"She needs to see a specialist," Tanya interjects. "This is more than a simple case of weak nerves."

Leo dismisses that with a hand wave. "Nonsense. Mama's health is fine. It's Father who's gone into a second childhood. He's completely under the influence of Chertkov. That scoundrel has built a royalty-free publishing house on the old fool's back."

"Still, accusing Father of homosexuality!" Sergey objects.

"Right, that was over the top. They are killing each other with slow torture. I don't know what to do except to separate them for a while."

A servant enters with Leo Junior's coat and hat.

"Is it time?" Leo asks.

The servant nods.

Leo gets up. "Got to catch the train." He slips into his coat. "Andrey's received my telegram. He's coming soon. So is Ilya. As for Misha, don't count on him. Too selfish to get involved."

He turns to Tanya. "Well, good-bye, soldier! I know you'll do your best."

In the carriage, the briefcase is discarded on the floor. Sonya leans against Bulgakov, still clutching his hand.

"Thirteen children and only seven left to me. The worst was Vanyechka. Such a bright boy, exactly like his father! I was mad with grief. And, only recently, Masha died. A short illness and she was gone. Gone forever."

Sonya finally releases Bulgakov's hand to search for a handkerchief. She dabs her eyes, weeping softly.

"We had a rich life. Rich in sorrow, rich in work. Do you know that I copied seven versions of War and Peace? Two million words. With the children and the estate to take care of all by myself. You know Leo Nikolayevich. He's brilliant but so impractical! It was a shock for me when he turned to sainthood. It's all right for him to renounce his wealth but he still comes and says, give me money for this and money for that. It does not occur to him that money has to come from somewhere. We had many disagreements over it. It's all in the diaries. Our whole life with its ups and downs. And a great love. Yes, a great love!"

She blows her nose. "You will not fail me, Valya, will you?"

"Of course not, Sophia Andreyevna."

"I used to be the person who kept the diaries. Tell Chertkov that if he gives them back to me, I'll grow calm again. I will like him again, and he can come to see us as he used to and we'll work together to serve Leo Nikolayevich. Will you tell him? For the love of God, will you tell him?"

Bulgakov swallows a tear and nods.

"Let him copy them all, every word! But at least, let him give my husband's original manuscripts back to me. Promise me you'll tell him!"

"I promise."

"I'm told that you have hitch-hiked with Sophia Andreyevna," Chertkov says. The news had reached his office before Bulgakov had.

"She offered it to me," the young man says. "She also entrusted me with a commission." He takes in a deep breath before saying passionately, "Vladimir Grigorievich, I beseech you to give in to her wishes. It's wrong to torture a sick old woman. The return of the diaries will bring peace to Yasnaya Polyana. Think of Leo Nikolayevich and the harassment he's going through."

"Do you mean to say that you came straight out and told her where the diaries were?" Chertkov accosts him.

Surprised by the fierceness of Chertkov's attitude, the young man steps back. "No, I couldn't tell her because I don't know where the diaries are."

Chertkov is seething. "Oh, now that's wonderful!" He strides toward the door and opens it. "Please, go now!"

Downstairs in Telyatinki, in a covered porch, tea is spread on a wicker table. Mrs. Chertkov is pouring a cup for Sonya.

"As far as I understand it, your husband entrusted the diaries to my son voluntarily," she says.

"My husband's an aged man. His decisions are no longer wise."

Her hostess shrugs. "It is not up to me to decide who is wise and who is not. The reason for my invitation was to discuss a more pressing point. It has been brought to my attention that you are spreading a most disgusting rumor about my son and your husband. Countess, my son is a good man. He does not deserve such an acute hostility. You must understand that under the circumstances, I shall not consider helping you in any matter whatsoever."

A hushed conversation is being held in Leo's study.

"So you will not meet him?" Goldenweiser asks.

The old man is contrite. "I'm sorry. I'm very sorry, but under the circumstances, with my wife on hunger strike and the family milling around the house, I can't have him here and I don't dare to visit Telyatinki. God knows what would happen if she hears about it."

"Still, Vladimir Grigorievich would prefer to settle the problem as soon as possible."

"What exactly is wrong with the will?"

"Just a few words but they must be written in your own hand. In fact, there's no need for you and Vladimir Grigorievich to meet. I could bring two reliable witnesses."

"All right, but not here. Let's keep it out of this house."

A quiet meadow is enlivened with the thunder of Leo's galloping horse. He reins in and waits, his patriarchal beard flying in the breeze.

Three somber riders: Goldenweiser and two Tolstoyan youths approach from the opposite direction. A short silence follows their meeting. Leo nervously scans the horizon.

"Let's not stay here in the open," he says.

The cloak-and-dagger riding party reaches a forest clearing. They ride about in circles, indecisive.

Goldenweiser is the first to speak. "That tree stump over there. What do you say?"

They dismount. Leo installs himself on the stump while Goldenweiser unpacks a writing pad, an ink bottle, and a pen.

"Let's get this over," Leo says.

The next morning, he and his two eldest children are lingering in front of Sonya's bedroom while a maid carrying a tray leaves the room.

"Did she eat her breakfast?" Leo asks.

The maid shakes her head and shows him the untouched food.

"Third day without food. You are going too far, Papa!" Sergey says.

Leo's looks at Tanya. She shakes her head with disapproval. With a nod, Leo acknowledges his defeat.

At Telyatinki, a stone-faced Sasha, accompanied by Varya, is handing a note to Chertkov.

"It has come to that!" she says.

As Chertkov scans the note, his benevolent expression hardens. He strides out of his office followed by the two women.

The Tolstoy factory is a large room with bookshelves containing files, publications, and Tolstoy memorabilia. The walls are hung with photographs and multi-language posters picturing Leo in various poses: reading to peasant children, making shoes, building haystacks, harvesting wheat. On a long table in the center, piles of pamphlets are awaiting expedition. Several typewriters are in action. Staff, both male and female, are stuffing and addressing envelopes.

Chertkov enters, followed by Sasha and Varya. He unlocks a cupboard and retrieves a pile of notebooks. He calls for attention.

"Listen, all! As you know, there's been a controversy concerning the custody of the Master's diaries. Unfortunately, worn out as he is by his wife's hysteria, he has given in to her demands. It means that should the diaries fall into Countess Tolstoy's hands, they would be heavily edited to safeguard her reputation. It is our duty to future generations to preserve Master's thoughts intact."

He begins to distribute the notebooks. "Let's all sit down and sift through the text. Any complaints or derogatory remarks involving the countess must be copied and archived. If we apply ourselves, we will be done by sundown."

There is a flurry of activity and scraping of chairs as the staff settles down to the task.

Chertkov indicates a chair to Sasha. "Won't you join us, Alexandra Leovna?"

After a short hesitation, Sasha accepts the invitation. Both she and Varya join in the effort.

Sunset has arrived at Yasnaya Polyana, the orange light warming the white tablecloth on the veranda. The samovar had been turned off; there are cake crumbs on the plates and a heap of ashes in the ashtray. Lounging at the table, are Ilya Tolstoy, Sergey, Tanya, and her husband, Sukhotin.

"Doctor Rossolino?" Ilya says. "Never heard of him."

"Professor Rossolino. Moscow Medical School. The best," says Sukhotin.

Ilya shakes his head. "Two specialists at the same time! Don't you think you're overdoing it? Mama's not that ill."

"A second opinion is important," Tanya says.

Ilya consults his watch. "What's taking the girls so long? And where's Mama?"

Mama is posted at the attic window, her eyes attached to a pair of binoculars. She is watching the road leading to Yasnaya Polyana. In the round image, she sees a carriage appear from the direction of Telyatinki.

The carriage has stopped in front of the house. Sasha and Varya are stepping out, both carrying parcels wrapped in brown paper.

Sonya shoots through the door and grabs the packages.

"Mama, you have no right!" Sasha exclaims.

Clutching the parcels in her arms, Sonya runs into the hall and begins to mount the steps with Sasha at her heels. Sasha grabs hold of Sonya's skirt and pulls her back. Sonya reaches for the rail to steady herself, dropping the parcels. The notebooks spill out of the torn paper. Two pairs of eager hands fight for the diaries.

"Mama, stop it this minute!"

Sonya gives her daughter a mighty push and gathers the diaries to her chest.

"Tanya! Sergey!" Sasha calls for help. "Come quick!"

In the salon, Sergey is rewrapping the diaries, while the other children cluster around Sonya's chair. Sonya is confused, she appears not to understand.

"Mama that was the deal," Tanya says, trying to be patient. "We are supposed to take them to the bank first thing in the morning."

"And the strongbox key?" Sonya asks. "You must give me the key!"

Sasha taps her forehead with her palm. "For God's sake, Mama! Don't you understand? Papa has made it clear enough. He will keep the key. He, and he alone!"

"Sasha, shut up!" Ilya says. "I won't have you shouting at Mother."

"Why can't I keep the key?" Sonya insists. "I want the key! What good is there in having the diaries if I cannot keep the key?" She looks beseechingly at her sons. "Seryozha? Ilya?"

The brothers sigh and shrug their shoulders. Sonya slowly rises from her chair, casts a last look at her children, and leaves the room. There is a long, guilty silence.

Leo emerges from his study with Sonya at his heels. "I can't," he says. "I can't. This is my last sacrifice."

Sonya falls to her knees, her hands clutching Leo's legs. "This is my last request. Give me the key! Give me the authorization to take the diaries! I don't believe that you won't return them to Chertkov."

Leo succeeds in freeing himself and escapes down the stairs. Sonya leans over the handrail.

"Why was I not allowed to see the diaries? What plots have you kept from me? Have you written a secret will?" She pauses as the truth dawns on her. She murmurs to herself: "My God, that's it! That's what it is about!"

Leo is visibly shaking. As he nears the last step, his legs give way and he lowers himself to sit. He hears his wife shout his name and winces.

"Leo!" she screams. "Leo, I have drunk a whole vial of opium!"

Leo is rushing toward Sonya, who stands in the door of her bedroom with her arms crossed.

"I said that to punish you. I didn't drink it."

Seething with rage after having been told what happened, Sasha strides toward Sonya's bedroom. She opens the door and shouts:

"He says that if you don't stop tormenting him, he'll leave. Why him? Why not you? Why not?"

At the railway station, Sonya paces along the platform, unaware of the curious looks her agonizing expression elicits from the waiting passengers.

There is a sharp whistle of an approaching train.

Sonya's stare is fixed on the rails. She steps to the edge of the platform, dangerously exposed to the coming locomotive. With a screech of brakes, tons of metal are careening closer and closer.

The rails are down there, waiting, as the noise grows until it envelops the platform.

Sonya jerks back and the iron monster lumbers past her.
Still under the shock of what could have been, she stands frozen while the train comes to a halt and the passengers begin to step down, Andrey among them.

"Mama?" He notices her suitcase. "Are you going somewhere? Mama, what are you doing here?"

"I don't know. I was told to leave."

"Oh, my God. Come! Come home!"

Part Three
The Promise

"How long have you suffered from insomnia?" Dr. Rossolino asks Sonya.

"Ever since Mr. Chertkov moved to Telyatinki. Mr. Chertkov has been the cause of all my sufferings."

The doctors are in Sonya's bedroom and Dr. Rossolino scribbles her answers in his notebook.

Dr. Nikitin takes out his watch. "Sophia Andreyevna, would you allow me to take your pulse?"

While Sonya rests in her room, the family and the doctors gather downstairs.

"The countess has a combination of hysteria and paranoia," Dr. Rossolino says. "The first shows itself in the especially vivid coloring of her experiences. The second is indicated by excessive suspicions and the forming of incorrect conclusions about her husband, his teachings, and his relationship with Mr. Chertkov."

"What kind of treatment do you recommend?" Tanya asks.

Later, she brings in her mother. "Come, Mamushka, have a seat!"

Sonya installs herself in an armchair. The family is watching her with anxiety.

"The doctors recommend that you and Papa should separate for a while. What do you think?"

"No." Sonya begins to weep. "Where would I go? Where do you want to send me?" She turns to Leo. "You planned it a long time ago, didn't you? The trip to the madhouse - was it to find out where to lock up your wife?"

"Nonsense," Leo mumbles. "Nonsense."

Tanya squats by the chair and takes her mother's hands. "Mama, nothing was planned. We only think that you two need a period of separation to calm your nerves."

"Ilya? Andreyusha? Sergey?"

"Mama, it will be for the best," Sergey answers. "You must admit that things are not working out here."

"All of you? . . . Leo?"

Leo makes an indecisive gesture.

"So I am to go to make way for Chertkov? Is that it? Don't you see, you fools? The moment I'm gone that scoundrel will have your father all to himself. He'll have it all, including what should come to you once your father's dead. Ask him! Ask him about the will! There's a will, I know it."

Leo springs up from his seat and begins to pace the room. "This is going nowhere. See what we are doing to her!" He turns to the doctors. "Is there another solution?"

"Sophia Andreyevna's nerves could benefit from frequent baths and long walks," says Dr. Nikitin.

"And a complete avoidance of stressful situations," adds Dr. Rossolino.

In the courtyard, a carriage is waiting while Tanya sees out the two physicians. Alone, in the door, Leo observes the scene.

"Idiots," he mumbles.

There is a smell of damp moss where sun rays are fighting their way through tree branches to land on two horses, one chestnut, the other gray. Holding the bridles, Leo and Chertkov stroll in the forest.

"Surely, we could arrange other meetings like this one," Chertkov says.

"No, this must be our last. Things are calmer now that I promised Sonya never to see you again."

"But surely, Leo Nikolayevich . . . "

Leo shakes his head in disagreement. "It was wrong of me to deceive my family about the will. I should have done it openly, or I should have left things as they were."

There is a hint of panic in Chertkov's voice: "Not so, Leo Nikolayevich, not so! You've done nothing wrong. You've simply obeyed the will of God by resisting your family's greed. I'm naturally concerned for your peace, and since Sophia Andreyevna asks you not to see me, I'll submit without a murmur."

Leo gratefully squeezes Chertkov's arm. "Sonya, too, has made a sacrifice. She's agreed to a separation. I'm going to live with Tanya - at least for a while."

Chertkov stops abruptly, forcing Leo to do the same. They stare at each other, both brimming with emotion. They squeeze each other in a farewell hug. Leo frees himself from Chertkov's arms and hastily mounts his horse.

He looks back at Chertkov. "I did promise not to see you. I did not promise not to write to you."

Chertkov smiles. "Every day!" He watches as Leo leaves, his smile quickly fading.

Night has descended upon Yasnaya Polyana. Two servants carry a trunk downstairs, where they add it to other pieces of luggage piled up by the door.

In the salon, Sonya weeps. "Please! I promise I'll behave."

Leo looks at Tanya and her husband. "I'm going to bed." Wearily, he gets up and leaves.

Sukhotin yawns. He nods toward the weeping Sonya and signals to Tanya to sooth the situation. "I'd better turn in as well. We have an early start."

"Everybody's betraying me!" Sonya wails. Sobbing, she runs out of the salon. They hear the main door slam.

Sukhotin rolls his eyes. "Jesus, not another hide-and-seek party tonight! I'm weary of these games. Where does she get the energy at her age?"

Holding her arm under the elbow, Tanya leads her mother upstairs. "It's only for a week, Mama. You both need a rest."

Sonya wiggles out of Tanya's grip. "A rest from what? A rest from my love, is that what you mean? What would you say if I took your husband away from you?"

"Mamushka, please, be reasonable! You've agreed that it would be for the best."

Sonya weeps again. "You are killing me, all of you! How am I supposed to get better if you keep wounding me mortally from all sides? I don't want to be left alone."

Her loud moans bring Leo out of his bedroom. "Let her come with us!" he says, exasperated.

Sitting on the balcony at Kotchety, Sonya and her granddaughter Tanyechka are dressing a doll. Rummaging in her sewing basket, Sonya retrieves a ribbon and ties it around the doll's hair.

"There! Isn't that pretty?"

After admiring the doll, Tanyechka hugs her grandmother. Sonya's arms tighten around the child.

A morning mist hangs over the garden. Clad in a dressing gown tied over her nightgown, Sonya cuts flowers and gathers them into a bouquet.

Leo is asleep when Sonya enters carrying her bouquet. She sits on the edge of the bed and tickles her husband's face with the flowers. "Lyovochka, my soul, wake up!"

Leo sneezes and opens his eyes.

"Good morning, Lyova! Guess what day is today? It's your birthday! You are eighty-two! I wish you all the best, my dear. Good health and long life to you!" She kisses her husband and goes on primly: "I mean a long life without deceptions, secrets, or obsessions. And I hope that now that we are friends again, you'll become truly enlightened."

Leo is not pleased.

Crumpled napkins and fading flower decorations. Empty plates, crumbs, and stains on the tablecloth. Wine glasses with traces of red liquid at the bottom are being carried away. A celebratory meal is coming to its end. Seated around the table are Leo, Sonya, Sasha, Tanya, Sukhotin, Dr. Makovitsky, Bulgakov, and Tanyechka. Valets are serving cake, tea, and liquor.

Leo takes a gulp of water. "Chastity is the Christian ideal and ought to be practiced by all," he says.

"Indeed, nothing is healthier both physically and mentally," Dr. Makovitsky chimes in.

Sonya sips her cognac. "I would disagree with that, Doctor. Why, Leo, when we were younger—not so long ago!—you claimed that without discharging your energy you could not write well."

Leo scowls. Sonya is blissfully unaware of the embarrassment around the table. "Besides, if we were all monks or ascetics there would be no children, and without children, there would be no Kingdom of God on earth."

Leo explodes. "What's the use of talking to you? You don't want to understand anything! You don't even listen!"

Sonya looks at the frowning faces around her and bites her lip. With tears in her eyes, she leaves the table.

She sits at the dressing table in her room, combing her hair, when Leo enters and hovers at her side.

"I came to say good night."

"Good night then." Sonya's tone is flat.

There is a tense pause. "Why did you leave the table?" Leo asks.

Sonya silently brushes her hair.

"I did not mean to shout at you," he says.

"Because of you, I became pregnant sixteen times. Thirteen children and three miscarriages. And you talk of chastity!"

"Sonya, I want peace."

"And what do you want me to do so that we can live in peace?"

"Abandon the copyrights, give the land away, and live in a cottage."

"All right, I agree with our going to live together in a cottage."

Leo swallows this surprising declaration and it does not agree with him. He puffs his cheeks. "For God's sake, leave me alone! I will go away! It's impossible to be happy if, like you, one hates one-half of the human race."

"But whom do I hate?"

"You hate Chertkov and me."

"Yes, I hate Chertkov, not you." Sonya's voice is rising. "I'll keep you two apart even if it means that I must kill him. Then come what may. As it is now, life is hell."

Carrying a folded newspaper, Bulgakov strides toward Leo, Dr. Makovitsky, and Sasha, who are ambling along a garden path, enjoying the early fall sunshine. He waves the newspaper to attract their attention. They meet to peruse an article. The news is good to judge from their smiles.

Tanyechka skips out of the house, followed by Tanya and Sonya. The readers split apart instantly. Sasha snatches the newspaper, hides it in the folds of her skirt and heads for the house. Leo pursues his morning stroll with a spring in his step.

Sonya's eagle eyes have not missed the scene. Furtively, she follows Sasha.

She stands at the foot of the staircase, listening to the sound of footsteps upstairs. Her head is tilting as she follows the progress of the noise. She hears the creak of an opening door. After a pause, the door closes, and the footfalls are heard again. Sasha is returning to the staircase.

Sonya slips away as Sasha appears on the landing.

In front of the house, Leo and Dr. Makovitsky rest on a bench. Leo is in a confiding mood.

"Yesterday, after reading a Maupassant story, an idea came to me to portray a spiritually alive person in the midst of vulgarity. It could be either a man or a woman. Oh, how great it could be, and how it attracts me! Maybe I shall do it." He sighs. "No, I think not. The struggle with Sonya saps my energy."

They watch Sukhotin returning from a ride. On the lawn, Tanyechka skips a rope while Tanya and Sasha chat.

"No!!! No!!! No!!!" It's Sonya's voice.

Sukhotin reins in his horse and hastily dismounts.

Sonya, clutching the newspaper, bursts out of the house. "This is my death sentence! I will not stand for it! I'll kill him! I'll pay someone to poison him!"

Frightened, Tanyechka drops the rope and runs for the shelter of her mother's arms.

"Do you hear me, Leo?" Sonya shouts. "I'll kill him and then I'll kill myself!" She collapses on the ground, moaning and convulsing.

Sukhotin is aghast. "What is this? What's happening?"

"Chertkov," Sasha explains. "There's a government notice that the ban has been lifted. He can remain at Telyatinki without depending on his mother's presence. It means that he is completely free." She points at her mother. "For God's sake, do something about her!"

Sukhotin seizes the weeping Sonya and drags her into the house. In the salon, he forces her into an armchair.

"Enough!"

Startled, Sonya clams up.

Sukhotin stands in front of her, legs apart, hands on his hips. "This must stop! Bear in mind, that if you go on destroying your husband, he will leave you. Your glory as Tolstoy's wife will collapse."

Sonya sweeps tears with her palms. "I will write to the papers. I will justify myself."

"That's where you're wrong. Rumors are already circulating about the shrew of Yasnaya Polyana. Too late to justify yourself. A man in his eighties does not leave his wife for nothing."

There is a pause as Sonya digests this fact.

"What's more," Sukhotin says, "I suspect that you are faking your mental illness."

"No, I'm really ill."

"If you are, then follow the doctors' advice. Part with Leo Nikolayevich. Otherwise, he'll be forced to leave you."

"If he does, I'll print a death letter in the papers about all he did, and then I'll poison myself and disgrace him all over Russia."

"But nobody will believe you. Nobody!"

Sonya's luggage is being loaded onto a waiting carriage. Sonya, at her meekest, is taking leave of her family. One by one, she embraces them, squeezing their hands, kissing the somewhat reluctant Tanyechka.

"Forgive me," she repeats with each hug and handshake. "Please forgive me . . . forgive me." She is addressing the servants: "Forgive me. Goodbye. Goodbye, all of you."

"Are you sure you want to travel alone?" Leo asks. "Sasha's willing to accompany you."

"No, alone. I must be alone."

Part Four
The Big Cleaning

Shortly after Sonya's return to Yasnaya Polyana, the big cleaning takes place. Varya, quietly strolling along a path close to the house, is startled as an object flies out of a window and crashes at her feet. She bends over to inspect it. It is a shattered framed photograph of Leo and Chertkov shaking hands.

Varya dodges two more projectiles: portraits of Chertkov and Sasha. Sonya appears at the window and spies Varya examining the debris.

"Leave that!" she orders.

The next day, a cloud of fragrant smoke wafts from Leo's study mingling with the sound of a religious chant. An Orthodox priest is sprinkling holy water over the room followed by an acolyte swinging an incenser. Sonya stands by, head bent over her joined hands, praying.

In his office, Chertkov listens to Varya's report. "She had the house exorcised to get rid of your evil spirit. She's plotting not only to inherit the early Tolstoy copyrights but to get hold of all Master's writings. She told me that everybody would believe her if she says they were written before 1881. And, if there's a will in your benefit, she and her sons will break it on the grounds of her husband's senility. She said that no man of sound mind would disinherit his family."

Chertkov appears satisfied with this new development. "Leo Nikolayevich must be made aware of this. I'll write to him immediately," he says.

The trees in Yasnaya Polyana are shedding their leaves. In the hall, Bulgakov's suitcase rests under the coat hanger. He is in the salon sitting across from Sonya and sipping tea.

"Eat the pierogi, they are freshly made, "Sonya says. "You must be starved."

Bulgakov gratefully reaches into the serving plate.

"Am I to believe that he's truly returning home?" Sonya asks. "His silence is hurtful. For weeks, I have received not a single word from him."

"Tomorrow, for sure."

"It will be a sad wedding anniversary. There is no joy left in this marriage. When I think back, when I remember the eighteen-year-old Sonyechka Behrs to whom he said: 'If you don't accept my offer of marriage, I'll shoot myself', when I remember that, I want to weep. To tell you the truth, I don't love him anymore. I think I don't. Before Chertkov appeared, we were man and wife. What are we now?"

"Sophia Andreyevna," Bulgakov offers timidly, "I think that, should you accept the fact that Master will never forget Mr. Chertkov, there could be hope for reconciliation."

Sonya shakes her head. "You naïve boy! I know that you mean well, but such an idea is simply inconceivable."

A gloomy silence accompanies the rattle of the carriage. On this night journey from the railway station, Leo is huddled in a corner, sharing the seat with Sasha. Dr. Makovitsky sits opposite.

"Are you feeling well?" the doctor asks.

Leo shrugs. "No, I cannot say that I am. I feel uncomfortable with the idea of what awaits me at home. It's impossible to talk to her. She is not bound by either logic, or conscience, or truth.

Not to speak of any love for me - she does not even need my love. She only needs that people should think that I love her. And that's terrible."

The three travelers have entered the hall and are divesting themselves of their coats. Sonya, wrapped in her dressing gown, slowly descends the steps. She and Leo look at each other in silence.

"Why didn't you come sooner?" she asks.

"Because I didn't want to."

Sonya turns her back to him to retrace her steps.

In the light of the day, Leo contemptuously stares at the wall in his study where the photographs of Chertkov and Sasha had hung. They are now replaced with Sonya's portrait.

On the gravel path in the park, Sonya drags Leo toward Bulgakov who stands behind a camera. "What do you mean by no? Are you refusing me what you accorded to your fancy friend? For him and his cronies, you pose like an old coquette. It's our forty-eighth anniversary. Surely, I am entitled to a record of this day."

She aligns her surly husband in front of the camera and, clutching his arm, sticks to his side. "Take the picture, Valya!"

While Bulgakov focuses the lens, Sonya notices that Leo has turned his head away from her. "Leo, look at me and smile!"

Thumbs tucked into his belt, Leo scowls and pulls away. Sonya jerks him back. She forces a smile and holds, while Leo doggedly maintains his surly expression. The camera shutter clicks.

Standing in the shade of the house, Sasha observes her parents with an angry frown.

In the office, Varya classifies files. Sasha sits in front of her typewriter, arms folded, brooding. Nobody moves when a bell rings in Leo's study.

"He wants you," Varya says.

Sasha tightens the fold of her arms.

"Are you not going to answer?"

Sasha shrugs.

The study door opens, and Leo pokes his head in. "Sashenka? I need you to take dictation."

No reaction from Sasha.

Varya discards the files. "I'll do it, Leo Nikolayevich."

Sasha stands up. "No! It's all right." She gathers a pencil and a notebook. Stone-faced, she enters the study.

"Sasha, what's wrong with you?" her father asks. "Are you not feeling well?"

She explodes. "I'm sick to my stomach, Papa, and that's the truth. I'm sick of watching you obeying her like a dog." She points at Sonya's portrait. "Look at that! Are you going to leave it there? My God, Father, have you no will of your own?"

"You are so much like her, Sasha."

Sasha gasps, startled by the truth of Leo's remark. She falls to her knees and wraps her arms around her father's legs.

"Forgive me, Papa! Please forgive me! I love you so much. She's not worthy of you. I can do so much better. Papushka, please, let's get out of here, just the two of us! Let's live in a hut, let's live a simple life the way you always wanted to! I'll wash your shirts, I'll scrub the floor, I'll take care of everything."

Leo gathers her in his arms and strokes her back. "Sasha, Sashenka . . . This is a beautiful dream. A dream! In reality, within days, Mama would move next door with her servants and fine china, and the situation would be much the same." Tears appear in his eyes. "All I need is your love, Daughter, just your love."

Sonya is clutching her throat. She is staring at a portrait of Chertkov that has replaced her own.

She yanks it off the wall. The glass breaks as she smashes the frame against Leo's desk. Varya and Bulgakov, both frozen with apprehension, watch as Sonya exits from Leo's study clutching the portrait.

She is brandishing the photograph at them. "He has re-hung it. You see? You see?"

She tears the photograph to bits. Looking at the scattered paper, she reconsiders, drops on her knees and gathers the shreds. "No . . . I must burn it. He must burn."

A small heap of ashes is smoldering in the fireplace. Sonya, brooding, sits on her bed, playing with a revolver. She aims at the fireplace and shoots.

In the courtyard, Leo and Dr. Makovitsky are dismounting from their horses. The household members led by Bulgakov and Varya gather around them. A discussion follows, during which Bulgakov mimics shooting.

"She says she was practicing," Bulgakov says.

Leo is reclining on the bed while Dr. Makovitsky removes his boots and massages his ankles. They both jump at the blast of another shot. Leo and the doctor exchange looks. Leo wearily shakes his head, lies down to rest and closes his eyes.

The final cleaning act takes place the same day. Coming from outside, Sasha and Varya encounter Sonya looming at the top of the staircase.

"Get out of my house, you two vipers!"

Sasha is stunned. "Mama?" she asks.

"Pack up and get out!"

Leo is stretched on the bed. "Where are you going?" he asks.

"To Telyatinki. There's a cottage to let," Sasha says.

"That's good. That way, you can still come every morning."

"But Papa . . . "

But Leo is exhausted. "It's good, it's good."

During Tanya's visit, only four people sit down at the dinner table.

"You fired your secretary?" Tanya asks. "Why?"

Sonya unfolds her napkin. "I suspect that Varya is in collusion with Chertkov. I'm not taking any more risks. As for Sasha, that, too, has been long coming. I cleaned out the vipers' nest. Now we have a true home. What takes Father so long? Someone, please call him! The soup is getting cold."

Bulgakov gets up. A minute later he charges down the staircase and into the dining room. "Doctor!" he shouts.

Leo is convulsing on the bed - face twisted, legs trashing. Makovitsky and Bulgakov hold him down with Tanya's assistance. Sonya is frozen with horror.

Another fit follows. Sonya falls on her knees. "Not this time, Oh, Lord! Not this time! Please spare him!"

Breathless, Sasha is rushing upstairs. She finds Leo undressed and tucked in, lying motionless. Dr. Makovitsky and Tanya keep watch over him while Sonya is praying on her knees.
Sasha stops by the bed and looks at her father. "How many convulsions so far?"

"Five," Tanya answers. "He's better now. He sleeps."

"I didn't want that," Sonya whispers. "I didn't want that!"

It's dawn. The evening meal is still on the table, untouched. Sasha enters and approaches the samovar. She pours tea and drinks thirstily.

Sonya steps in. "The tea is cold."

"I know."

"Sasha?"

"Yes, Mama?"

"I know I was wrong."

"Were you, Mama?" The question is heavy with sarcasm.

"I shouldn't have thrown you out. Please forgive me and come back."

"No, thank you. We are very well, Varya and I."

"She can come too. She can have her job back. I'll do anything to make Father better. Anything! Let's unite to make his last days peaceful. Even Chertkov can visit him."

Leo sits on the bed, his back propped against several pillows. Sonya puts a tray with food on his lap.

"You really don't remember?"

"No. I felt a little tired, so I took a nap. When I woke up, there were a number of anxious people around the bed."

Sonya sits on the bed, takes his hand and kisses it tenderly. "Are you well enough? If you wish to see him tonight, I'll send an invitation to Telyatinki."

Leo grins happily.

Later that evening, Sonya sits in an armchair, hands in her lap, waiting. She hears the trot of an arriving horse. Her back begins to bend under the stress. She clasps her hands over her head, becoming a motionless knot.

Bulgakov, carrying his briefcase, is intercepted by Sonya. "Are you going to Telyatinki?"

"Yes, Sophia Andreyevna."

Sonya folds her arms in an uneasy embrace. "Last night I tried to reconcile myself with the idea of accepting Vladimir Grigorievich under my roof. Believe me, I tried. But I simply cannot endure his presence. When he was here, I felt I was dying. So please, tell him that he must come no more."

Sonya is undressing when Leo enters her bedroom. He takes a determined posture. "Wife, I want to talk to you, and I beg you to listen to me without interruption."

This conversation soon ends in the corridor, where Sonya pursues her retreating husband. "Don't try to hoodwink me into thinking that he's no closer to you than your own family!" she shouts.

"I will not have him here - not ever! - and if you want peace at home, you'll stop seeing him. Do you hear me?"

Leo chooses not to answer.

"I will not sleep until I find the truth about you two," Sonya adds as parting words.

At dawn, the stable hand brings Leo's horse. As Leo is about to mount, Sonya exits the house.

"Where are you going?" she asks.

"For a ride."

"You are going to see Chertkov."

"No, I'm simply going for a ride."

"That's a lie. I know you are going to see him."

Leo shrugs and swings his leg over the horse's back. "Believe what you want."

It is a cold, gloomy day for a ride. A blustery wind agitates Leo's beard as his horse trots along the road. A rattle of wheels alerts him that he is not alone. He turns to see Sonya driving a dog-cart. Having not wasted time to fetch a coat, she is shivering in her house dress.

Leo reins in his horse. Sonya does the same. They stare at each other defiantly before Leo nudges his horse forward. Sonya follows, maintaining the same distance. Periodically turning his head to see what his wife is up to, Leo leaves the road and urges his horse across the fields. With grim determination, Sonya keeps following him over the uneven ground.

The chase ends back at the mansion. Leo dismounts and starts toward the house as Sonya's dog-cart arrives. Stiff with cold, she alights with great difficulty. Leo walks home without sparing her a glance.

Leo is staring through the open door into the salon. He is observing his wife who, sneezing and coughing, sits on the sofa wrapped in a blanket. She is warming her hands around a steaming mug of tea.

Leo comes in and selects a pear from a fruit basket. He cuts it in half and arranges it on a dessert plate. He carries the offering to Sonya. Sonya accepts one-half and hands him the other one. Sitting side by side, they munch on their fruit.

Part Five
The Flight

Leo enters his room and wearily sits on the bed. After a pause, he moves to the desk and lifts the lid of the inkstand. He reaches into a pair of old boots under the desk. His arm stiffens. Turning the boots upside down, he shakes them, but nothing comes out. He rummages in the drawers without success. Dejected, he looks around the room.

Bulgakov, seated at the desk in the office, lifts his head as Leo enters.

"Have you, by any chance, seen a red notebook anywhere?" the old man asks.

"No, I have not. Do you want me to look for it?"

Leo is silent. Bulgakov acknowledges the air of tension. "What was it, Leo Nikolayevich?"

"A diary. A diary for myself alone."

In the moonlight, Leo stares at the ceiling of his bedroom. He hears the door opening in the adjoining study and props himself on his elbows. A beam of light appears under the door. Furtive steps move around the room, drawers are being opened and closed. He hears a rustle of paper, a creak of a cabinet door.

The steps approach the door of Leo's room. He falls back in his bed, pretending to be asleep. The door opens. Holding a lamp, Sonya stands on the threshold and observes her husband. Satisfied, she gently closes the door.

Leo listens to her retreating steps. In the ensuing silence, he throws off the cover, steps into his slippers and tiptoes to his daughter's bedroom. His hand gently grips Sasha's shoulder. She wakes up with a start.

"What . . . ? Papa? Papa, what's wrong?"

"Shhh . . . Don't make noise! Sashenka, I'm leaving here. I'm leaving Yasnaya Polyana."

In the dark and silent house lights appear: one window, two, three. In Leo's room, a feverish packing is in progress. Varya and Sasha, both nervous, struggle with the lids of over-packed suitcases. Varya's finger gets caught in the lid. She lets out a yelp of pain.

Wincing, Sasha puts a finger across her mouth. "Shhh! Quiet, for God's sake!"

The old man, outwardly calm, stacks manuscripts into a case. Dr. Makovitsky, watch in hand, tries to get hold of his wrist.

Leo yanks his hand out of the doctor's grip. "There's no time for that."

Makovitsky succeeds in taking his pulse. "One hundred. I'm not sure this is a good idea."

Leo shrugs him off. A suitcase slides from the bed with a loud thump. All activity stops. A moment of tension follows as they listen for any sound in the house.

In the feeble moonlight, Varya and Dr. Makovitsky haul luggage onto a waiting wagon. Sasha stumbles into her father who, down on his knees, is frantically searching along the path.

"My cap, the wool one. I've lost it."

"Leave it! " Sasha says. "I'll get you another one."

The platform at the railway station is deserted except for Leo and Dr. Makovitsky, who placidly waits by the luggage. Wringing his hands, Leo paces back and forth. "I wonder which will come first. The locomotive or Sonya?"

In the mansion, Sonya descends the steps when Sasha, holding an envelope, appears at the foot of the staircase. "Good morning, Mama," she says. "This is for you."

Puzzled, Sonya reaches for the envelope.

Bulgakov is approaching the front door when it flies open, and a wild-eyed Sonya bursts out. Sasha appears in the doorframe. Hopping on one foot and pulling a galosh on the other, she notices the startled Bulgakov.

"Go after her!" she orders. She returns to the house screaming for help.

Bulgakov sprints along a path. Behind him, Sasha and two male servants have joined the chase. They see a flash of gray dress between the bushes. "She's going to the pond!"

Sonya, running, has reached the pond jetty with Bulgakov not far behind. She scurries along the plank, slips on the wet surface and falls. Seeing Bulgakov coming at her, she does not waste time to get up. Instead, she crawls toward the edge and clutching at the plank, she rolls into the water.

Bulgakov dives in. Grabbing Sonya by the shoulders, he drags her toward the shore. Sasha and the two men splash waist-deep in water. They reach Sonya and hoist her up. A group of spectators has formed around the rescuers as they half-drag, half-carry Sonya toward the house.

Clutching the handrail of the open platform of a railway carriage, Leo is happily exposing his face to the wind as the countryside runs past him. Dr. Makovitsky joins him.

"Leo Nikolayevich, I must insist. Do come inside at once or you'll catch your death!"

Leo grins at him. "Freedom, Dushan! Freedom!"

In his office, Chertkov is beaming. "Yes! Yes! At last! Well done! How soon can I join him? Where has he gone?"

"Only Alexandra Leovna knows," Bulgakov says. "You can contact him through her."

"And the countess?"

Bulgakov shakes his head. "Four attempts at suicide. But we watched her closely. Now there are a doctor and a nurse keeping an eye on her around the clock. It's a tragic situation. So sad. Everything is sad." He hands a letter to Chertkov. "She begs you to come. She wants reconciliation."

Chertkov takes this with a smug smile. "Does she now? I don't think I'll oblige."

Bulgakov looks at him with disdain. "So you've done it, Vladimir Grigorievich. You've won the war. I hope you're satisfied."

Chertkov opens his mouth to speak, but Bulgakov lifts his hand to silence him. "I had the greatest respect for you, Vladimir Grigorievich, but I'm no longer naïve. You could have stopped this tragedy by giving back the diaries. You could have allowed the trusting old man to live his last days in peace, but that would mean sharing your power over him and his legacy. I don't know much, but one thing I know perfectly well. You are not his friend."

A nurse holding a tray with food hovers over Sonya. The latter, draped in a dressing gown, her hair in disarray, is stretched on Leo's bed, hugging an embroidered pillow.

"Lyovochka, where are you? Are you well? Where are you laying your head tonight? Speak to me, my love! Distance means nothing between us."

"Sophia Andreyevna, if you don't eat this time, the family is considering force-feeding."

"Why has he done this to me? Isn't it written in the gospels that a man should never abandon his wife? . . . He's a brute! He could not have acted with more cruelty. He meant to kill me!"

The coat rack in the hall is weighted down with numerous coats and hats. A servant is carrying suitcases upstairs. The emergency family reunion takes place in the salon. Present are Sasha, Tanya, Sergey, Ilya, and Andrey. The youngest son, Mikhail, is seated at the piano, performing a light-hearted waltz.

"And Lyova?" Ilya asks. "Is he going to show up?"

"He's still in Paris. He must have received my telegram by now," Sasha says.

"Well, what do you expect us to do?"

"Why, support Papa's decision, of course."

Ilya frowns. "I suppose we should admire him for trying to kill Mother. This situation is the result of your machinations, Sasha. You and Mama have been at odds ever since Ivan died. You just couldn't forgive a grief-stricken woman, could you?"

"Forgive for what?" Sergey asks.

"Don't you know?" says Andrey. "The day Vanya died Mother supposedly cried 'Why Vanyechka? Why not Sasha?' The servants talked. Maybe it's true, maybe not. The fact is that Sasha has carried the grudge too far."

"That's not true!" Sasha exclaims. "How dare you accuse me of plotting against Mother? My only concern was for Papa. Before you criticize me, have a good look at yourself! You broke your parents' hearts when you ran away with the governor's wife. Papa left only because he could no longer endure this kind of life."

Andrey waves his hand in dismissal. "Oh yes, his eternal complaints against a life of luxury! I say that if he could endure it until now, he could have gone on for the last few years as well. What about Mama? Hasn't she suffered enough?"

"Absolutely," Ilya says. "She'd never think of deserting him. She'd bear her cross to the very end. He's a selfish man. Very selfish. Can you imagine how this will play in the press? All that bad publicity for our family and Mother in particular!"

Tanya disagrees with him. "He did what he had to do. I'll never condemn him. How about you, Sergey?"

"I cannot begrudge him the desire to conserve his sanity. The fact is that Mama is ill and in many ways irresponsible. I wish she could change, but she never will."

"I propose that each of us write Papa a letter expressing our feelings," Tanya says. She turns to Mikhail. "Misha?"

Mikhail, still playing, simply shrugs. Sasha approaches the piano and slams the lid on Mikhail's hands. He yelps with pain.

"Now that we have your attention, will you write to Papa?" Tanya asks.

"Why should I write to him? He knows I don't like to write."

In the long majestic corridor of the Shamardino convent, Leo strolls in the company of his sister Marya.

"I couldn't go any farther without saying farewell to you," he says. "And now that I'm here, I feel I have arrived. I spent the night at the monastery and enjoyed the profound peace. There was cabbage soup for dinner. What else do I need? If the brothers allow an old apostate like me among them, I'll stay. After all, are we not all truth-seekers each in his own way? Does it matter if we take a different path to God?" Leo gently strokes the old nun's shriveled hand. "You don't condemn me, Marya, do you? Please say you don't!"

Marya squeezes his wrist. "I never stood in judgment of you. You know that, Leo."

"Being here with you is like going back in time, like drinking from the fountain of our happy childhood."

Marya smiles at him.

Sitting on the bed in the hotel room, Leo struggles with his boots. Dr. Makovitsky makes a move to help him.

"Don't! I can take care of myself."

He makes another ineffective attempt at removing his boots and finally surrenders to Makovitsky's care.

The door opens to admit Sasha and Varya with their luggage. Both are bundled up against the cold.

"Papa! Thank God! What weather!"

Leo looks at his daughter apprehensively. "What's going on down there?"

"I have letters for you. Papa, you cannot stay here. Mama has figured out you'd stop at the convent to see Aunt Marya. We must move on."

"But I don't want to move on. I don't want to think of it now."

"He's tired, Alexandra Leovna," Dr. Makovitsky says. "He needs rest. Why don't we leave him to his letters?"

Reluctantly, Sasha hands over a bundle of envelopes. "Please, Papa, be strong! Don't give in! Do you know what Mama said? She said that as soon as she gets you back, she'll never let you out of her sight."

In Dr. Makovitsky's room, Sasha, Varya and the doctor bend over a map.

"If we go, we must know where we're going," he says.

Sasha ponders her answer for a while. "That depends on whether we'd be able to obtain passports. I've been thinking of Bulgaria or Turkey. If not, then there's the Caucasus. It has a healthy climate."

Leo, alone, sits hunched over a pile of opened letters with one of them hanging out of his hand. Misery keeps him company.

In the other room, the trio now studies the railway timetable. "There's a train going south at seven forty in the morning," Sasha says.

Dr. Makovitsky has his doubts. "How do you expect to pull it off? We're looking at some thirty hours on the road with the most famous man in Russia. He did not pass unnoticed on his way here."

"I've thought of that. The best way to cover our tracks is to buy tickets in succession along the way."

Leo enters, the letters in hand.

"Papa! How would you like to visit Cousin Olga in Novocherkask? We'll stay for a few days and take our bearings."

Leo has other thoughts in his mind. "Only Tanya and Sergey are giving me their blessings."

"Papushka, you're not giving up, are you? If we stay here, they'll hunt you down, you know. They'll set the police on you. They'll say that you act erratically because you're senile, or some nonsense of the sort."

"I must send my thanks to Sergey and Tanya. And I must answer your mother's letter."

Sasha looks at him questioningly.

"No, I'm not going home," Leo says. To himself, he adds: "Not yet."

Part Six
The Terminus

The train carriage is packed with passengers, many of them reading newspapers. As Sasha passes through, a pair of middle-class men cannot contain their amusement.

"A neat little trick the old boy played on his wife! Packed up in the night and ran away."

"And after she had taken care of him all her life. I'd say he didn't care for her care!"

Sasha takes it in with a mixture of dismay and bitterness. When she reaches her compartment, she finds Leo stretched on the bench. He is coughing and fighting for breath while Varya and Dr. Makovitsky tuck a blanket around him.

"Everything's known," Sasha says. "The papers are full of it."

Dr. Makovitsky looks at her, his face grave with concern. "Alexandra Leovna, I'm afraid your father's not doing well."

The train is chugging through the vast isolation of the flat steppe. In the corridor, an assembly of curious passengers is staring through the glass door of a compartment. A soldier is elbowing his way through.

"What's going on?"

"It's Tolstoy. Papushka Tolstoy's here, on this train!"

Standing on his toes to gain a better view, the soldier joins the peeking group.

The train comes to a halt. A large number of passengers step down, leaving their luggage behind. Leading the crowd, an anxious Sasha accosts the stationmaster. Pointing toward the village, she asks him a question. The stationmaster shakes his head. He waves his arm, indicating that the refuge she is seeking is far away down along the line. Sasha is on the verge of crying.

Several bystanders join in, gesturing toward the train and imparting The Information. The station master's countenance changes abruptly. With subservient diligence, he points to a small house nearby.

The crowd returns to the train, forming a human hedge at a door. Helpful hands stretch up as Leo, supported by Varya and Dr. Makovitsky, appears in the door frame. A blanket wrapped around his shoulders, his head lolling, he is handed down and slowly led toward the house. Hats and caps are lowered as he passes through the solemn, silent crowd.

An onlooker is watching with great interest. He detaches himself from the spectacle and heads for the telegraph office.

At sunrise, a motley crowd of laborers, peasants, and reporters besiege the station master's little house. At the railway station, the window of the telegraph office is open. A lone employee deals with customers clamoring for his services.

At dusk, a train is stationed by the platform, the locomotive steaming. Spilling out of the wagons is a Pathé Cinematograph team with their equipment, several doctors, a gaggle of nurses, a murder of church dignitaries in their raven-black robes and hats, and a school of shark-like reporters. An oxygen canister and a hospital bed are handed down from the baggage wagon and carried toward the little house.

The small station is bursting at the seams. Numerous tents have been erected on both sides of the platform. Visitors without the protection of the tents rest around makeshift fires. The telegraph office is now equipped with additional apparatus manned by four employees.

A journalist, a pencil behind his ear, stands at the street entrance to the station. His attention has been caught by something in the street. He is joined by a reporter waving a telegraph strip.

"Orlov, this Tolstoy business is getting out of hand!" the man shouts. "The tsar has curtailed his holiday in Germany and returns home. The government smells a revolution. I bet they are shitting in their pants."

Orlov smiles and motions toward the street. A detachment of cavalry is quietly surrounding the station.

His colleague is awed. "Oh, shit!"

Orlov chuckles. "Russia has two tsars, and one of them is here. The clergy is circling the old apostate's deathbed like vultures, hoping for a moment of weakness. So far, they have been shown the door. Now enters the army. One key element is missing though."

"What?"

"Countess Tolstoy, of course. I wonder why? Without her, the drama's not complete. Could it be that she alone doesn't know the whereabouts of her husband? Dear colleague, we must remedy the situation. Let's send the good woman a telegram."

At night, a locomotive pulling a lone Pullman car is speeding along the tracks with Sonya inside. Surrounded by her children, she hugs Leo's embroidered pillow.

"It's not too far now," Tanya says.

Sonya sighs. "Five hundred rubles for a special train! When this is over, I'll make sure it never happens again. In the future, where he goes, I'll go. Andreyusha, read that once more!"

Andrey unfolds a newspaper. "Temperature 104, inflammation of the left lung confirmed. A persistent attack of hiccups has been treated with a solution of sugared milk and soda."

Sonya shakes her head in disapproval. "They should have spread hot goose fat on his chest. I'll see to that." She reacts to a screech of brakes. "Have we arrived?"

As the train is coming to a stop, hundreds of flaming torches pass in front of the window. "What is this?" Sonya stammers. "What is this?"

A sea of torches surrounds the train. A crowd of thousands, mostly workers and peasants, fill the station with prayers and chanting. In the Pullman car window, Sonya watches this multitude with horror.

The Tolstoy family is getting ready for the ordeal. The bewildered Sonya makes the sign of the cross and clutches the pillow to her chest. The door swings open and a tumult of voices assaults the party. Helped by her sons, Sonya descends the steps, fearfully eyeing the pack of reporters that have surrounded the wagon.

She is assaulted by countless questions. "Countess Tolstoy! Is it true that you have attempted suicide? . . . Are you hoping to reconcile with Leo Nikolayevich? . . . Countess Tolstoy, what is your side of the story?"

Sonya opens her mouth. "I ..."

Ilya steps in. "No, Mama, not a word! . . . No comment. No comment! Let us pass!"

With the help of the police, a path is cleared for the Tolstoy family. Sonya sees a hedge of grim faces and accusing stares, she feels an atmosphere of silent hostility.

The entrance of the station master's house is guarded by two faithful Tolstoyans: Sergeyenko and Goldenweiser. At the approach of the Tolstoy family, Goldenweiser disappears into the house. Sergeyenko blocks the door.

Andrey frowns. "What is this? Do you deny us the access to husband and father?"

"Just obeying doctor's orders, sir. He will be with you shortly."

"We will not stand for it. Step aside!"

Before this can turn into a serious dispute, Dr. Makovitsky and Sasha fill the entrance.

"Please, please!" the doctor pleads. "No raised voices, I beg you! Leo Nikolayevich is unaware that his refuge is known to you. We'll have to break the news to him gently."

The door closes, and Sergeyenko resumes his vigil. Condemned to wait outside, the Tolstoys are uneasily aware of the silent crowd behind them. Finally, the door opens, and Dr. Makovitsky steps outside.

"It's all right. He will see the children."

"And Mother?" Ilya asks.

"I'm sorry, Sophia Andreyevna, but not you."

Andrey steps forward. "What are you saying?"

The doctor is humble. "Andrey Leovitch, I beg you again not to raise your voice! The sight of her would send your father into a shock." He breaks into tears. "He's so fragile, so fragile . . ."

They all look at Sonya, who begins to understand the gravity of the situation. Tanya is first to break the silence.

"Mama, I'm sorry but you should wait here." She kisses her mother and enters the house.

Ashamed, Andrey says: "So sorry, Mama," and follows his sister.

Ilya hugs his mother. "We won't be long."

One by one, her children abandon Sonya. The door shuts closed. The crowd returns to chanting and prayers. Left alone with the grim-faced Sergeyenko, Sonya approaches the window. Raising herself on her toes, she peers inside. She sees that the room is full of people she detests: the Tolstoyans. As her children enter, the occupants step aside to let them pass. A path opens to Leo's bed.

Sitting by her husband, holding his hand, is Chertkov.

Sasha steps close to the window. She looks coldly at her mother and mercilessly draws the curtains.

Leo Nikolayevich Tolstoy died at 6:05 in the morning of Sunday, November 7, 1910. His wife was not allowed to see him until after he had lapsed into a final coma.

"Wrong does not cease to be wrong because the majority share in it."

"A quiet secluded life in the country, with the possibility of being useful to people to whom it is easy to do good, and who are not accustomed to have it done to them; then work which one hopes may be of some use; then rest, nature, books, music, love for one's neighbor — such is my idea of happiness."

"In the name of God, stop a moment, cease your work, look around you."

"We can know only that we know nothing. And that is the highest degree of human wisdom."

"A man can live and be healthy without killing animals for food; therefore, if he eats meat, he participates in taking animal life merely for the sake of his appetite. And to act so is immoral."

"Freethinkers are those who are willing to use their minds without prejudice and without fearing to understand things that clash with their own customs, privileges, or beliefs. This state of mind is not common, but it is essential for right thinking..."

"Rummaging in our souls, we often dig up something that ought to have lain there unnoticed."

"All the variety, all the charm, all the beauty of life is made up of light and shadow."

"Everyone thinks of changing the world, but no one thinks of changing himself."

"If you look for perfection, you'll never be content."

"It is amazing how complete is the delusion that beauty is goodness."

"The two most powerful warriors are patience and time."

"Only people who are capable of loving strongly can also suffer great sorrow, but this same necessity of loving serves to counteract their grief and heals them."

"Respect was invented to cover the empty place where love should be."

"If it is true that there are as many minds as there are heads, then there are as many kinds of love as there are hearts."

"Nothing is so necessary for a young man as the company of intelligent women."

"When you love someone, you love the person as they are, and not as you'd like them to be."

"If everyone fought for their own convictions there would be no war."

"If you want to be happy, be."

About the Author

Iva Polansky authored several non-fiction books and the novel *Fame and Infamy* set in the 1870's Paris. She lives close to the Canadian Rockies and you can meet her on her blog *Victorian Paris*.

Is it hard to be famous in 1870's Paris? Ask the sharp-shooting contest winner Miss Nelly McKay, formerly of Butte, Montana. She is already walking the thin line between fame and infamy when she is noticed by Chancellor Bismarck and the German Secret Service. Yet all she ever wanted was to marry a gentleman!

Fame and Infamy is an entertaining blend of comedy, mystery, romance and hard facts. Sarah Bernhardt and Victor Hugo are among the celebrities who share the scene with gritty characters emerging from the bohemian Latin Quarter. Paris, mopping up after the twin calamities of war and. revolution, provides a background for this hearty clash of French and American cultures.

Amazon Reviews

A beautifully written journey into historic Paris
[...]In all, Fame and Infamy is a vastly entertaining, beautifully written excursion into the memorable world of historic Paris, and its success is amplified by wonderfully detailed history, richly drawn characters - both heroes and villains - and a plot that will keep the reader guessing until the end.

A Compelling Story with Broad Appeal
As a man, I might have missed the opportunity to escape into the fictional world presented in Fame and Infamy; I might have chosen to forgo reading of the highs and lows of Miss Nelly McKay in Paris. But something reigned in my attention, something not unlike the fascination I felt while watching the Ernest Hemingway portrayal in the film Midnight in Paris.
Iva Polansky's novel is a rich read, full of complex and captivating characters. From Nelly's encounter with the Widow Koenig, a fierce entrepreneur who agrees to hide Nelly's endangered identity, along with the sympathetic boy Zidore, I was hooked. From there, I became submerged in nineteenth century Parisian life, from its grit to its high life; I was compelled along by the unfolding mystery. Fame and Infamy has all it takes to appeal to a

wide audience. The story rewards; the conclusion satisfies.

Chapter One

Usually, no one paid undue attention to the Chinese laundry, a squat clapboard building with misted windows. This Saturday afternoon however, the laundry's entrance door was being surveyed from the Happy End Saloon across the muddy main street. A dozen men in various states of ruggedness lounged about on the covered porch, glasses of beer at reach, puffs of tobacco smoke swirling above their heads.
"Sure Miss McKay's there?"
"Sure, Mitch. Saw her goin' in with a big basket of laundry."
"Sure she likes me?"
"Hey, Pete, you saw the look she gave Mitch last Saturday, didn't you?"
"And a mighty lusty look it was. She turned around to take him from behind the rump too. I'm tellin' ya, she's ripe for the pickin'."
"Pete's right, Mitch. This is your opportunity. Why wait another week?"
"O.K. then, I'll try."
"You do that, boy. You do that. Just squeeze her hard and give her a kiss."
Mitch detached himself from the wall, straightened his hat and ambled across the street.
Soft chuckles followed his departure.
The saloon keeper appeared in the door frame. "You're at it

again, guys," he said disapprovingly. "That poor ignorant fool."
"Oh, c'mon, it's harmless fun."
"It's harmless as long as she shoots under the feet. One day she might miss and do real damage."
"She's never missed, has she?"
"Can't say she has."
"Never, so far."
"Nah, never..."

After a short hesitation, Mitch entered the laundry. The crew in front of the Happy End saloon craned their necks, awaiting the upcoming entertainment. Nothing happened for thirty seconds. Then the door opened and Mitch backed out, hands in the air. He was staring into the shining barrel of a nickel-plated Colt Bisley, first prize in the local sharp-shooting competition. Clutching the revolver was Miss Cornelia McKay, her other hand dragging an empty laundry basket. Passers-by going about their business stopped in their tracks.
Miss McKay aimed at Mitch's feet, ready to pull the trigger, when a premature laugh drew her gaze in the direction of the saloon and the assembly of hoodlums, all of them beaming in anticipation. Mitch profited from the distraction by taking flight along the wooden sidewalk. With the traffic at a standstill, the clatter of his boots was the only noise in the street. Everyone expected well-aimed projectiles to enliven Mitch's escape but it didn't happen. Not this time.
Five rapid-fire bullets shattered beer glasses. The sixth removed a hat from Pete's head and broke the saloon window behind him.
With the chambers empty, Miss McKay lowered the smoking revolver. She surveyed the glass shards scattered in the puddles of beer, the ashen faces, the sweaty brows and shaking hands.
"I hate this town," she said. "I really hate this town."

Later that afternoon, in the private quarters of the printer's shop farther down the main street, a conference was in progress.
"You must admit, Angus, your niece has become a real problem," said Sheriff Selby. "You know I hate arresting her, but this time I had no choice. Public safety and all."

"It's odd that you should mention public safety, Ned," said Angus McKay. "A young woman should be able to move around freely without being molested."

The sheriff moistened his moustache in a cup of tea served by Angus's wife Teata, who sat with them at the kitchen table with a thumb-sucking toddler in her diminished lap. The latest McKay, thirteenth in succession, was expected to draw first breath in a few weeks time.

"I can't be everywhere," the sheriff complained. "Butte is a gold-mining town crammed with randy bachelors ... pardon my French, ma'am, but that's a fact. Any single female's fair play. You can't change that. If only Miss Nelly would get married, that would put an end to this."

"Married!" Teata exclaimed, her cheeks coloring with anger. "She's just refused Mr. Frobisher's offer. Had she accepted, she could have owned the general store. She could have worn silk to church and our family would have been able to buy fruit again. Today, he got a shipment of prunes and before I got there, they were gone. Since she's humiliated him, he no longer puts anything aside for us. There's nowhere else to shop and God knows what will happen when we get snowed in for months on end. He may even deny us flour for bread."

"That I doubt, Mrs. McKay. Still, your niece seems to have unrealistic expectations. What went wrong this time?"

"According to her, the man has no conversation. He grunts instead of speaking. Now that wouldn't do, would it? Miss must have conversation. That's what they filled her head with in that fancy boarding school back East. French! Piano playing! Money wasted, if you ask me."

"My brother meant well," Angus said. "An only child growing up without a mother and him always on the road, what else could he have done?"

Teata turned to him. "He should've put money aside for her upkeep instead of gambling it away and then getting himself killed. That's what he should've done instead of hanging her around your neck like a dead weight. A pig-headed lass who expects to marry a gentleman! That's not going to happen in Butte."

"You're right, Mrs. McKay," said the sheriff. "I propose the most convenient solution, which is that Miss Nelly should leave Butte for a location where there's a sufficient supply of gentlemen."

"Now look here, Ned Selby!" exclaimed Angus. "If you think I'm going to send my niece away to fend for herself just to save you the effort of keeping order in town, you are very much mistaken. It's my duty to look after my kin."

The sheriff put the tea cup back on its saucer with a clink. "Your kin's only a hair away from supplying bodies for the undertaker. We can't have that."

"I can't keep her inside, Ned. The girl does have a right to fresh air."

"That she does. Only there's an opportunity for her to breathe fresh air away from Butte. A once in a lifetime opportunity."

Angus frowned. "Ned, I told you—"

"Listen to the sheriff, husband," Teata interrupted him. She eyed Ned Selby eagerly. "An opportunity, you said?"

"That's so, ma'am. You heard about the folks who are staying at the hotel?"

"The heiress from the East and her French husband? Everybody talks about them. Only a crazy Frenchman would drag his wife to a place like Butte. Exploring the Wild West, he calls it. With a valet and a maid! And the poor woman so exhausted that she had to take to bed."

"She's mended now but they need a new maid. The one they came with has left them. Up and married. Can't blame the gal. She's nearing forty and by her looks, she's never had such a choice of eager grooms."

"Don't you see, Angus?" Teata said. "There's a hand of destiny in this."

Angus barred her enthusiasm with his ink-stained hand. "Not so fast, wife. We don't know these people. And Nelly must decide for herself."

"That she's already done and she's got the job," said Sheriff Selby. "All that's required of you, Angus, is to write a witnessed permission allowing the Frenchies to travel with an unrelated minor."

"Nelly's set you up, hasn't she, Ned? She's talked you into this."
"Write that permission, husband!"
"Your wife's right. You can do no wrong by signing. It's best for everybody," the sheriff urged.

Months later, when the newspapers from the East reached Butte after the spring thaw, those words came to haunt him. By that time, the *De Chazelle Murder Affair* had made the rounds of the civilized world.

(406 pages. Available in print and in Kindle version.)

Proof

Made in the USA
Columbia, SC
24 January 2018